HOWARD CARTER

SEARCHING FOR KING TUT

HOWARD CARTER

SEARCHING FOR KING TUT

BY BARBARA FORD

ILLUSTRATED BY JANET HAMLIN

Scientific
American

BOOKS FOR YOUNG READERS

W. H. FREEMAN AND COMPANY ◆ NEW YORK

Book design by Debora Smith

Scientific American Books for Young Readers is an imprint of
W. H. Freeman and Company, 41 Madison Avenue
New York, New York, 10010

Library of Congress Cataloging-in-Publication Data

Ford, Barbara

Howard Carter: searching for King Tut / by Barbara Ford

p. cm.

Includes index

ISBN 0-7167-6587-x.—ISBN 0-7167-6588-8 (pbk.)

1. Carter, Howard, 1873-1939—Juvenile literature. 2. Tutankhamen, King of Egypt—Tomb—Juvenile literature. 3. Egyptologists—Great Britain—Biography—Juvenile literature. I. Title.

PJ1064.C3F67 1995

932'.007202—dc20

[B]   94-36730

CIP

AC

Printed in the United States of America

10 9 8 7 6 5 4 3 2 1

CONTENTS

CHAPTER 1

†

The Boy and the King

Eight-year-old Howard Carter was amazed. He had never seen anything like it before: a long case in the shape of a human body. A mummy had been inside it, his older brother explained. And not just any mummy. It was the mummy of an Egyptian king who ruled Egypt 3,500 years ago. Mummies were the bodies of dead Egyptians, dried out with chemicals and wrapped in bandages to protect them in the afterlife.

It was the fall of 1882, and the Carter brothers were visiting an Egyptian exhibit at Didlington Hall, the huge English estate of Lord and Lady Amherst. The Amhersts owned the best private collection of ancient Egyptian objects in England. The objects had been excavated—dug up—by archaeologists, scientists who learn about the past from the remains of past civilizations.

Howard couldn't forget what he had seen. The eyes of the coffin had seemed to gaze right at him. Egypt! He had never thought about that distant land before, but now he longed to see it. Even the word was full of mystery and promise.

But as young as he was, Howard knew he had no reason to expect he would ever see Egypt.

Samuel Carter, Howard's father, was a successful artist who painted animals. Wealthy people paid Samuel Carter to make "portraits" of their pets. But Samuel and his wife had eight children, and there was no money for luxuries such as foreign travel. Howard's brothers and sister had begun working in their midteens. Several of them were artists like their father.

Howard, the youngest child, wanted to be an artist, too. His father was giving him art lessons. The lessons were special events for Howard, because they gave him the chance to be with his father. Samuel lived in London most of the year with his wife and all their children—except Howard. Howard spent most of his time in the small town of Swaffham with his aunts. For Howard, it was almost as if he were an only child—or an orphan.

Howard never knew for sure, but there may have been good reasons for his being brought up in Swaffham. Before he was born, three other Carter children had died as infants. Howard was a sickly baby, and his parents probably thought that a country town like Swaffham would be a healthier place for him than London, where the air was choked with pollution.

When Howard was old enough to go to school, his aunts thought he was too sickly to attend the local grammar school. Instead, he went to a small school run by local women. Such informal schools as this one taught children to read, write, and do simple arithmetic—but not much more. Although Howard was very bright, for the rest of his life he would have trouble with spelling and punctuation.

Because of Howard's poor health, his aunts warned him against playing rough games with boys his age. The result was that Howard never made any friends. And since his brothers and sisters were usually in London, he spent most of his free time by himself, roaming the fields and woods around Swaffham, making sketches of the animals he saw.

Howard quickly developed a love of nature that would last throughout his life. But being by himself so often also made him uncomfortable with other people. Even as an adult, Howard preferred to spend most of his time alone.

Growing up in Swaffham seems to have been good for Howard's health. Or perhaps he was never as sickly as his parents had feared. By the time he was a teenager, he was healthy—stocky, with broad shoulders and a strong jaw. His dark eyes gave him a "serious" look that was noted by people who knew him.

About this time, Samuel began visiting Didlington Hall again. He was probably painting an animal scene for Lord Amherst, who already owned a number of Samuel's works. The painter took his youngest son with him. At eight, Howard had been amazed by the Egyptian collection at Didlington, but the teenage Howard was consumed by it.

Lord Amherst noted Howard's serious interest and gave him permission to visit the collection and to use his library. Drawings and watercolor paintings of ancient Egyptian treasures soon filled Howard's notebook.

Howard's old desire to see Egypt was stronger than ever. But Egypt was as remote as ever for a boy who had to work for his living. At fifteen, he began working as a professional artist. Later, looking back on his early career, he wrote, "For a living, I began by drawing in water colors and colored chalks portraits of pet parrots, cats and snappy, smelly lapdogs. Although I was always a great lover of birds and animals . . . how I hated that particular species known as lapdog."

Then, early in 1891, Howard's parents visited him in Swaffham. They told Howard that Lady Amherst had come to see them. The Egyptian Exploration Fund, which excavated ancient sites in Egypt, needed an artist to trace and color paintings. Lady Amherst had already shown Howard's work to her friends in the fund, who wanted to know if he would be interested in the job.

Would he be interested?!

By May of 1891, it was settled. Howard would work as an artist—"tracer" was the official title—for one year for the sum of fifty pounds, about two thousand dollars. Summers in Egypt were very hot, so he wouldn't start work until late fall. First, he would spend the summer at the British Museum, becoming familiar with the Egyptian collection.

At the museum, Howard met members of the Egyptian Exploration Fund. Most of them were university graduates. They came from families with good connections in English society and spoke in very proper "Oxford English." Howard's middle-class Norfolk accent sounded strange at the stately museum, and his boots squeaked down its silent halls.

But Howard was quietly confident about one thing: his art. From the beginning, he felt he understood Egyptian art, and even though it was as different as possible from lapdogs and squawking parrots, Howard was immediately able to draw and color the strange scenes and figures.

The members of the Egyptian Exploration Fund praised his work, and Howard's confidence rose even further. He could do this!

In October, Samuel Carter saw Howard off at Victoria Railway Station in London. As the steam train puffed out of the station, Howard, seventeen years old, was alone once more. But he was on his way to the land he had dreamed of for so many years.

CHAPTER 2

☥

Friends and Foes

The Egypt that Howard Carter arrived in had been under the control of England since 1882. For a brief time before that, England and France had ruled Egypt together. The Antiquities Service, which controlled all archaeological excavation in Egypt, was headed by a Frenchman. Tensions among the British, the French, and the Egyptians ran high.

Howard knew all this, but he had little interest in politics. Just a few days after his arrival in Egypt, he was already at work tracing paintings from the walls of ancient tombs carved in cliffs above the Nile River. Tracing was not an exciting job for an artist. But Howard was so pleased to be in the land of his dreams that he hardly minded. Soon he was put to work making colored copies of the best paintings.

His copying work lasted for only a few months that first season. Then he went to work for British archaeologist Flinders Petrie. But not as an artist. Petrie was excavating a huge site—an entire city called Amarna. He was willing to train an inexperienced young worker in return for help with the excavation. Lord Amherst, who was paying for part of the excavation, had suggested Howard for the project.

Petrie is sometimes called the father of scientific archaeology in Egypt. In the past, archaeologists had dug carelessly, searching only

for large, valuable objects. But Petrie dug carefully, noting the exact location of each item. He passed up nothing. Small fragments of pottery that other archaeologists would have tossed out Petrie used as clues to ancient cultures. Howard credited Petrie with making him into an archaeologist. "He taught us the ABC of archaeological research and excavation," he said.

At Amarna, Howard was soon uncovering parts of stone carvings and other ancient objects. He enjoyed excavating, he found. The methods he had to use to get the job done appealed to his practical side, and as an artist he was drawn to the beauty of the objects he found. As Howard worked, he began to learn Arabic, the language of the Egyptian workmen who did the heavy labor.

One day, Petrie handed Howard a black-bordered letter. Inside was the news that Samuel Carter, at fifty-seven, had died of a stroke. In the journal he began keeping in Egypt, Howard says little about the death of his father. Howard respected Samuel as an artist. But having grown up away from his family, he was never close to his parents, so Howard was not as sad as he might have been.

When he went home that summer, Howard had a new goal. He still wanted to draw and paint Egypt's ancient treasures. But now he wanted to be like Flinders Petrie. And at that time, even an uneducated young man like Howard Carter could have such a dream. There was no formal training in archaeology. People who had studied the history, art, or ancient written language of Egypt took part in excavations as Howard had. They learned on the job. If they were skillful and lucky, they might even get to try their own "dig," as an archaeological excavation was called.

The next season, in the fall of 1893, Howard painted at the rock tombs again. At the end of the season, he was appointed chief artist at the Egyptian Exploration Fund's main dig. It was a temple built by Hatshepsut, a mighty queen who had taken control of Egypt from her stepson, who was too young to rule. It was near the Valley of the Kings, where many Egyptian kings were buried in tombs. Edouard Naville, a Swiss archaeologist, was in charge of the project.

There was so much to do at the site that Howard Carter the artist sometimes became Howard Carter the superintendent. He directed the Egyptian work crews who were excavating and restoring structures. Naville was very pleased with Howard's work. "He has a very quick eye for finding the places where the stones belong," Naville said. "Besides, as he has a thorough command of Arabic, he can direct and superintend the men."

Naville respected Howard's skills so much that, in 1897, he made him supervisor of all reconstruction work. Howard was still drawing and painting a record of the sculptures found on the temple walls. By this time, books on the rock tombs had been published with many of Howard's drawings and paintings, and experts praised his work.

When he wasn't painting or working for Naville, Howard explored the Valley of the Kings. The known tombs had been excavated, but every one had been robbed long before. Howard often went through the empty tombs, carrying a candle to see the paintings and sculptures on the walls. Howard now realized what he really wanted—to excavate in the Valley of the Kings. Perhaps he might even find a tomb that had not been robbed!

But to excavate, he needed money—or a partner with money.

In 1899, Gaston Maspero, the French head of the Antiquities Service, appointed Howard inspector of antiquities for upper Egypt. Howard was the only candidate for the job without a university education, but Maspero was sure he could do it. For an inspector, he needed someone with practical skills to oversee the excavation and preservation of ancient sites. This was just what Howard had been doing for the Egypt Exploration Fund. Maspero observed that Howard was "very active, a very good young man." But, he added, "a little obstinate."

The Valley of the Kings was part of Howard's district. One of the first things he did was to put up iron gates at the tombs' entrances to stop thieves. Tomb robbery was still going on in the Valley of the Kings. For the convenience of tourists, he installed electric lights in the tombs. He even set up a donkey "parking lot" where people could leave the animals they rode to reach the valley.

Howard's new job made him an instant hit in Egypt. Near the valley was the modern city of Luxor, which was built on the site of the ancient capital of Egypt, called Thebes. Many wealthy people from Europe and America spent the winter there. Howard began receiving

invitations to teas, dinners, and fancy parties. Little by little, he grew more comfortable with people. When he talked to his new friends about archaeology and art, they listened. Howard was an expert now.

In 1900, the Antiquities Service gave Howard the money to excavate a tomb on his own. He had literally stumbled onto the tomb while riding his horse near the Valley of the Kings. The top room of the tomb was empty, but there was a rubbish-filled shaft leading downward. There must be a mummy down there, thought Howard. And treasures, too! He was so sure of this he invited several officials to attend the opening of the bottom room.

But when the room was finally opened, it was bare except for a few pots. There was not even an empty coffin.

Deeply embarrassed, Howard would never forget this awful day.

But he pressed on. In 1902, he and his wealthy friend Theodore Davis agreed to start an excavation, this time right in the valley. Davis had a concession from the Antiquities Services to dig in the valley. This meant only he could excavate there. Davis, a lawyer, knew little about excavation. But he had money to hire the very best experts— like Howard Carter.

In two years, they found two royal tombs, but both had been robbed long before. There were only a few objects left inside.

Davis was intrigued enough to keep digging, but Howard had been transferred to the north to become inspector of lower Egypt. Sadly, Davis and Carter parted company.

In January 1905, a short time after Howard's transfer, some French tourists were visiting the famous monuments at the ancient burial site of Saqqara. According to the Egyptian guards, several tourists tried to get in without paying. A dispute developed and Howard was called. He sided with the guards and told them to escort the French tourists out of the monument. There was a scuffle, and at least one Frenchman and several guards were injured.

No one was seriously hurt, but Howard soon found that he had become front-page news in Egypt. The politics he had tried to ignore

now threatened his work. The French counsel demanded that action be taken against him. The English high commissioner set up an investigation. Gaston Maspero suggested, in gracious words, that Howard give not an apology but an expression of "regret" to the French counsel. But Maspero was about to find out just how "obstinate" Howard could be.

Despite the urgings of Maspero and Theodore Davis, Howard refused to give in to the French counsel. It was all very simple, in his eyes: he was right, the French were wrong.

Maspero decided reluctantly that he had to discipline Howard to avoid a real international crisis. He made Howard inspector of a much smaller part of lower Egypt. Howard spent an uncomfortable few months headquartered in a small town. The plumbing in his house didn't work, the weather was unusually hot, and there was nothing like Luxor's social life to take his mind off his troubles.

Howard was so unhappy that in October 1905, he wrote a letter to Maspero:

> Owing to the late treatment I have received and the difficulties I now find while endeavoring to carry out my duties as Inspector in chief in lower Egypt in the Service des Antiquités, I beg herewith to submit my resignation.
>   Believe me
>   Sir
>   Yours Faithfully
>   Howard Carter.

CHAPTER 3

$\dagger$

In the Valley of the Kings

At the age of thirty, Howard was out of work for the first time in fifteen years. He moved back to Luxor, close to the place he loved best: the Valley of the Kings. But now, when he visited the valley and nearby sites, it was as a paid guide for rich tourists. In one month in 1906, for instance, he took several members of a wealthy American family around Hatshepsut's temple, where he had once supervised whole work crews.

To make ends meet, Howard became an antiquities dealer, buying and selling ancient art and other items. He would continue this sideline throughout his life. He also sold his paintings to tourists.

While Howard was struggling to make a living in Luxor, the Earl of Carnarvon was excavating nearby. Lord Carnarvon, as he was called, was a very rich Englishman. Although he was only forty years old, the earl was in poor health and he had come to Egypt for the warm weather. He quickly became interested in archaeology.

For two years, Lord Carnarvon had excavated around Luxor without much to show for it except the mummy of a cat. In 1908, he asked Gaston Maspero to suggest an archaeologist he could hire.

He knew just the one, said Maspero, who still thought highly of the stubborn young man he had hired. Howard Carter.

So in 1909, Carter and Carnarvon, two very different men, joined forces at Lord Carnarvon's dig near the Valley of the Kings. Howard felt so secure in Carnarvon's employment that in 1910 he built a small house near the valley with bricks from Carnarvon's brick-making works back in England. People called the house "Castle Carter."

By this time, Howard and Carnarvon, with eight years difference in their ages and a much bigger difference in their backgrounds, were friends. Carnarvon was a sociable, confident man, the kind who always knew what to say in any situation. He was tall, thin, and elegant. If anyone *looked* like an earl, it was Carnarvon.

Howard, still awkward in society, must have been impressed with Carnarvon's easy manner. He certainly found the earl's elegance impressive. Before long, people noticed that Howard was dressing just like his patron. The earl wore bow ties and so did Howard. The earl wore well-cut suits in heavy fabrics even when the temperature went above a hundred degrees, and so did Howard. He bought the suits from the earl's tailor in London. Howard even put his cigarette in a holder the way Carnarvon did.

Carnarvon respected Howard's knowledge of Egypt and archaeology. When the earl wanted to try a new site, Howard convinced him that the Valley of the Kings was the place for them.

Theodore Davis still held the concession there. But by 1913, he was convinced that he could find nothing more in the valley. Davis turned the concession back to the Antiquities Service, which gave it to Carnarvon.

At last Howard was back in the valley, with the money to undertake a full-scale dig. But in 1914, World War I broke out in Europe. All excavation work in Egypt stopped as resources from all over the world were used for the war effort. Howard was forty, too old to serve in the armed forces. So he had plenty of free time—time to develop a plan for what he would do when the war was over. He read through every account of excavations in the valley.

As he read, he filled a notebook with his small, neat handwriting. Then he made a large-scale map of the valley that showed the site of each and every excavation and what had been found there.

As he read about Theodore Davis's excavations, Howard noticed there was one name that kept appearing. In 1906, not far from the tomb of Ramses VI, Davis had found a blue cup with the name of an obscure king, Tutankhamen. The following year, in the same area, he had found pieces of gold foil with the same name. Later, in the same area, Davis had found pottery jars stuffed with an odd assortment of items. One jar was wrapped in a cloth bearing the name of Tutankhamen.

Howard knew that only three kings from the Eighteenth Dynasty—the period when the valley was used as a royal graveyard—

had not been found. One was Tutankhamen. Little was known about this king, who had died at a young age in the fourteenth century b.c., more than three thousand years ago. But he was believed to be the son-in-law of Akhenaton, the king who had built Amarna.

Was King Tutankhamen buried in the Valley of the Kings?

The mystery of Tutankhamen gnawed at Howard, but he kept the name to himself. In 1917, he wrote Carnarvon, saying that the best place to dig would be in a triangle that could be drawn from the tomb of Ramses VI to the tombs of Ramses II and Merneptah. His plan was to remove everything above ground, right down to the bedrock. That way they could not miss a tomb.

In the fall of 1917, Howard began the difficult task of clearing the site. Practically the entire valley was covered with the rubble of earlier excavations, including stone chips from the original tomb builders. Archaeologists like Howard had to remove tons of this rubble before they could start their own excavations.

That first year, Howard's workmen removed debris around Ramses VI's tomb. Near the tomb they found the remains of ancient huts. The huts had probably been put up in the time of Ramses, who reigned after Tutankhamen, and used by workmen who built the tomb of Ramses VI. Closing off the area to remove the huts would prevent visitors from reaching Ramses's tomb, which was a popular tourist attraction.

So Howard decided to remove the huts later, after the tourist season.

Year after year, for six years, his workmen dug. By 1922, they had reached bedrock everywhere except in one place: under the workmen's huts. But once again, the tourist season had started. So once again, Howard put off removing the huts so he wouldn't interfere with the tourists. The season, like the others, had been disappointing. They had found practically nothing. Worse, before Carnarvon left Egypt that year, he told Howard that he wasn't sure whether he could continue to finance the dig.

CHAPTER 4

The Tomb of the Golden Bird

In June 1922, Howard Carter traveled to Highclere Castle in England to visit Lord Carnarvon. The two men were going to discuss the future of their dig in the valley. Howard was prepared to argue his case. With him he had the large map he had made showing the location of every tomb that had been excavated in the valley.

Carnarvon explained to Howard that he had already spent fifty thousand pounds—two million dollars—on the project. It was hard for him to continue supporting a dig when almost nothing was being found.

With a voice full of regret, he said that he could no longer finance the excavation in the Valley of the Kings.

But Howard was prepared. He swiftly unrolled his map. True, he said, almost all of the valley had already been excavated either by themselves or earlier archaeologists. But one small spot still remained to be explored, the area near the entrance to the tomb of Ramses VI that was covered by the work huts.

Howard proposed to return to Egypt in the fall, *before* the tourist season. He would remove the huts and dig down to bedrock. Then, and only then, would he feel that their work in the valley had been completed.

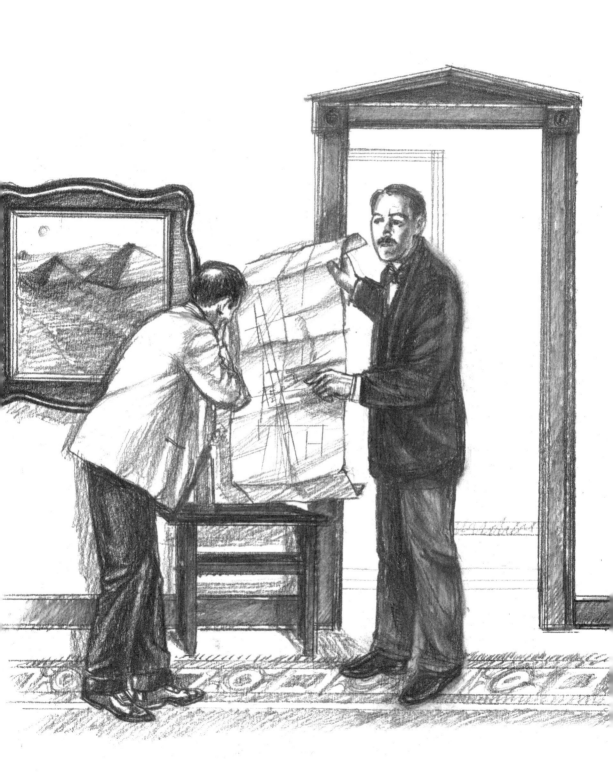

For the first time, Howard told Carnarvon that he was looking for a specific king. His survey of the records, he said, showed that only a few kings who had been buried in the valley had not been found. One of them was Tutankhamen. It was his name that had been written on objects found near Ramses's tomb. Howard felt that Tutankhamen's tomb was nearby.

Rolling up his map, Howard made Carnarvon an offer. Howard would pay the expenses of a short season to explore the area below the huts. But he needed to use Carnarvon's concession rights.

It was an offer that the earl, who considered himself a sportsman, could not refuse. So in October of 1922, Howard left for Egypt. He arrived in Luxor on October 27th with a new pet he had bought in

Cairo—a canary. His Egyptian servants had never seen one, and they were delighted with the little yellow bird.

"It is a bird of gold that will bring luck," they said.

While Howard was still in England, a new antiquities law had been passed in Egypt. Before this, excavators in Egypt could keep half of what they found. Under the new law, everything would go to the Cairo Museum. In a short time, Egypt would become an independent state, and Egyptians wanted to keep in Egypt what was dug up there.

Howard had been expecting the new law, and he was prepared to work under it. He would do almost anything to finish what he had started.

For this season, Howard assembled a hundred workmen, most of whom he had worked with for many years. He also hired Arthur Callender, a technical specialist whom he knew from his early days in Egypt, to help with details. The crew's first job was to remove the huts. Then they would dig down through the soil to the bedrock, which lay about three feet below the surface.

On November 1, the digging began. By the evening of November 3, the workmen had removed a group of huts. The next morning, they would begin to remove the rock and soil.

Work had usually begun at the site before Howard arrived by donkey from Castle Carter. Voices and the sounds of the *tureeya*—a combination of spade and hoe used for both farming and excavating—would reach Howard as he neared the site. As he rode toward the site on the morning of November 4, however, he heard nothing. Soon he saw why. The workmen were clustered together, peering into a trench.

A foreman stepped forward. They had found something—a step cut in the rock.

The news struck Howard like a thunderbolt. Most tombs in the valley had stairways that had been cut into the rock. He ordered the workmen to continue clearing. Another step appeared and then another. It was a steep stairway, very similar to those Howard had seen in valley tombs. Trying to control his excitement, he paced around the site, watching the workmen. In spite of their fast pace, it took until the late afternoon of November 5 to clear eleven steps.

As the sun was setting and the men were digging out a twelfth step, something caught Howard's eye. He rushed down the cleared steps. Before him was the upper part of a doorway, blocked, plastered, and sealed.

In the fading light, he searched the door for clues, but found no name. He did, however, recognize a familiar seal that he had seen on royal tombs in the valley, indicating that the tomb had been con-

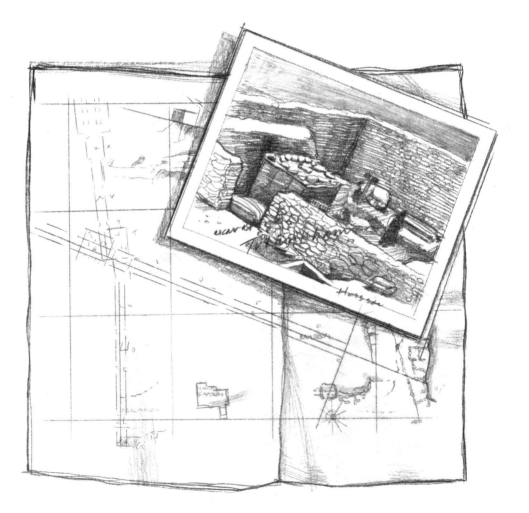

structed for a very important person. But the opening was small compared to that of the average king's tomb in the valley. Perhaps the tomb was that of a high-ranking official.

The door had a wooden lintel, a horizontal beam above the opening. Howard made a small peephole in the wood. The space beyond the door was filled with rubble. It must be the passageway to the tomb itself, he thought.

The moon was already rising. Howard selected his most trustworthy workmen to guard the tomb. Then he rode home by moonlight. What had he found? A hiding place for treasures from other tombs? The tomb of a nobleman? Or the tomb of that little-known king, Tutankhamen? And if it was the last, had it been robbed? He burned to know the answers. But in fairness to Carnarvon, he would delay opening the tomb until Carnarvon arrived.

The next day, November 6, Howard rode to the telegraph office in Luxor and sent a telegram:

AT LAST HAVE MADE WONDERFUL DISCOVERY IN VALLEY: A MAGNIFICENT TOMB WITH SEALS INTACT: RE-COVERED SAME FOR YOUR ARRIVAL; CONGRATULATIONS. CARTER.

Then Howard returned to the tomb and had his workmen cover the site again, so Carnarvon could see it in its undisturbed state. The workmen were convinced that Howard's canary had led them to the discovery, so they named the site the Tomb of the Golden Bird.

It took until November 23 for Carnarvon and his twenty-year-old daughter, Lady Evelyn, to arrive at Luxor by ship and train. The Carnarvons, Callender, and Howard were all at the site on November 24. By that afternoon, all sixteen steps of the staircase were clear. The sealed doorway was now completely exposed.

Howard stooped down to examine the lower part of the door, which he hadn't been able to see before. Here the seal impressions on the plaster were much clearer and he had no trouble making out a name.

Tutankhamen!

The name appeared in several places, Howard told his delighted audience. But then he noticed something else. The door appeared to have been opened and reclosed twice. The openings must mean that Tutankhamen had not escaped the tomb robbers any more than the better-known kings who were buried nearby.

He found something even more upsetting when he examined the rubbish the workers had removed from the staircase. The names of a number of kings appeared on fragments of pottery and boxes. Perhaps this *was* a hiding place for treasures robbed from other tombs.

Howard was so shaken by the thought of further robberies that he slept in the tomb that night.

On the morning of November 25, Howard helped the workmen remove the plaster-covered stones that had been used to block the door. Behind the door was a passageway that sloped downward. It was filled with rubble. In the middle of the afternoon of November 26, the workmen reached the end of the thirty-foot-long passageway. Facing them was another sealed door much like the first.

Inspecting the door, Howard found Tutankhamen's seal again. He also found signs of opening and reclosing. Howard feared even more strongly that they had found an empty tomb, one that had been robbed like all the others that had been found in the valley. But the crew kept working. Soon the whole door was revealed. Howard made a small hole in the upper left hand corner and pushed an iron rod through. The rod moved up and down freely.

The meaning of that was clear to everyone. There was nothing but blank space on the other side of the door. They had reached the tomb. Widening the hole a little, Howard put a candle though it. At first he saw nothing, but then, as his eyes became accustomed to the gloom, details began to appear. Speechless with amazement, Howard stood frozen and just stared.

Carnarvon broke the silence. "Can you see anything?"

"Yes," said Howard at last. "Wonderful things."

CHAPTER 5

☥

Wonderful Things

Howard made the hole in the door a little larger. He and the Carnarvons and Callender took turns looking through. The details of the room seemed to appear out of a mist. Strange animals, statues, shrines, vases, boxes. And gold—gold everywhere. "The first impression suggested the property room of an opera of a vanished civilization," he wrote in his notebook.

It was already late. Howard closed the hole and locked the padlocks on the outer door. Then, leaving the workmen on guard, he and the others rode their donkeys back to Luxor.

Howard later wrote a book about his famous find, *The Tomb of Tutankhamen*. The book tells how the group returned to the tomb the next morning. What it doesn't tell, though, is that Howard, Carnarvon, Lady Evelyn, and Callender returned to the tomb *that night!* The information about the secret visit only came out years afterward. On this night visit, Howard enlarged the opening in the second door. Then they slipped through, one by one.

The first things Howard noticed inside were the weird beasts carved on the posts of three beds, their heads throwing grotesque

shadows on the wall behind them. Piled haphazardly on and around the beds were boxes, vases, and black-painted shrines. Under one of the beds was a throne. A heap of chariot parts lay against one wall. Everything looked as if it had been dropped where it was in a hurry, without thought.

Two life-size black statues caught Howard's attention. They were dressed as kings, and on each one's head was a carved cobra, a symbol of the Egyptian kings. The statues faced each other against a wall as if guarding something.

Looking under one of the beds, Howard and his friends saw a low opening in another wall. The opening led into another, smaller room, even messier than the one they were in. Hundreds of objects, most of them small, were jumbled together in a heap covering every inch of floor space.

They had found a great deal in these two rooms. But there was no coffin, no mummy. If this was a king's tomb, where was the king?

Could the two black statues hold the secret? Howard examined the wall between them with a flashlight. At the bottom of the wall was what looked like a hole that had been resealed. Howard was sure the burial room lay on the other side of the wall.

Howard and his party removed the resealed portion of the door. Then he and the Carnarvons squeezed through the small opening and found themselves facing a solid gold wall. It was part of a shrine so big it filled up almost the entire room.

Howard knew Egyptian kings' coffins were enclosed in such shrines. But was there a king inside this one?

On one end of the shrine were big doors, bolted shut. In his book, Howard wrote about opening the doors for the first time months afterward. But he really looked inside the shrine earlier, probably that very night. "Eagerly we drew the bolts," he wrote, "swung back the doors and there within was a second shrine with similar bolted doors and on the bolts a seal, intact. . . . We felt we were in the presence of the dead king."

The inner shrine had not been opened. The king had to be inside! Howard closed the outer doors as quietly as he could.

There was a small room off the burial room with a black, life-size statue of the jackal god Anubis in the doorway. But they didn't have time to inspect it, so they wriggled back through the hole and blocked it up again, placing a basket lid and some reeds in front of the hole to hide it from view.

Years later, when word got out about the secret visit, some suspected that Howard and the Carnarvons took items from the tomb before anyone else saw it. But there was probably a simpler reason for the nighttime visit. In 1900, Howard had invited officials to the opening of the tomb he had found near the valley. He still remembered the humiliation of the moment when they discovered only an empty tomb. This time, he would make sure of what he had found.

On November 29, the tomb was formally opened to a small group of officials. Callender had connected the tomb to the electrical system installed by Howard twenty-two years before. The officials and a reporter from the London *Times* filed into the Antechamber, as the first room had been named. No one was permitted beyond it. Howard gave the reporter an account of the discovery of King Tutankhamen.

The next day, a two-page story and photographs appeared in the *Times* under the headline:

AN EGYPTIAN TREASURE: GREAT FIND AT THEBES.

The report touched off what came to be called "Tutmania." Reporters from all over the world flocked to the Valley of the Kings, swamping the Luxor telegraph office with reports to be sent back to their hometown papers. The tomb was a page-one story almost everywhere. Photographs made Howard's mustache and Carnarvon's hat familiar to millions.

With the reporters came tourists. It was the winter season in Egypt and every vacationer seemed to have put the valley on his or her schedule. They took all the hotel rooms in Luxor and headed for the valley in great caravans of donkeys. And some required personal attention—high officials, friends of Carnarvon, royalty. Howard spent much of his precious time conducting tours of the tomb for these important people, even though he had the biggest job of his life on his hands. Howard knew he needed help.

The Metropolitan Museum of Art in New York City was sponsoring an excavation nearby. Howard cabled the Met with a request for a photographer. The Met not only lent him Harry Burton, who

would take most of the photographs of the tomb, but two artists and Arthur Mace, an expert on ancient materials.

Work started in early December in the Antechamber. Only when it was cleared, Howard announced, would the blocked door be opened. Clearing was slow work. Flinders Petrie had taught Howard well: not only did each item have to be removed with great care, but the place where it was found had to be noted.

Howard put all the information on cards, one for each item, often including a sketch as well. It was the first time a tomb in the valley had been documented in such a thorough, scientific way.

An American Egyptologist, James Breasted, provided valuable help in the first stage of the work. He found that all of the seals in the tomb were from Tutankhamen's reign—including the ones on the resealed holes. That meant robbers had entered the tomb shortly after the king's death. The government officials who tidied up after the break-in were in a rush, so they ignored much of the mess. Then they resealed the tomb. No one had been in the tomb for over three thousand years.

While the Antechamber was being cleared, one of Howard's workers went to Castle Carter. As he came up to the house, he heard the cry of a bird. Inside he found Howard's canary in the mouth of a cobra. Egyptians living near the valley had no doubt what the canary's death meant: The cobra, a symbol of the Egyptian kings, had taken revenge on the bird for revealing King Tutankhamen's tomb. And the people were convinced that more terrible things would follow.

CHAPTER 6

✝

The Curse

Thanks to all the expert help he had, Howard was able to clear the Antechamber in just two months. He set the date of the official opening of the burial room for February 16, 1923.

But just when things seemed to be going smoothly, the team Howard had put together began to fall apart.

The trouble started with the two artists lent by the Metropolitan Museum of Art. They began having loud, angry arguments with Howard. One artist quit in February. The other team members were finding Howard hard to get along with, too. "That man Carter is quite impossible!" proclaimed Harry Burton.

In the excavations he had conducted before, Howard had done things exactly the way he wanted. Now, even though he was still in charge, he was part of a team. He had to adjust to the work habits of other experts. He was also under constant pressure from tourists and the press. Howard had a quick temper even under ordinary conditions—and there was nothing ordinary about working at the tomb. By February he was very tense. Arthur Mace even confided to his wife that he thought Howard would have a nervous breakdown.

For the opening on February 16, Howard had invited a group of about twenty officials and archaeologists. The London *Times* reporter was the only newsman. Carnarvon had signed a contract with the *Times* that gave them "exclusives" on any news that developed at the tomb. The guests sat on chairs in the Antechamber as Howard and Carnarvon took down the blocked up wall, stone by stone.

Howard and Carnarvon already knew—from their night visit months before—what was behind the wall, but they played their parts well. Everything went perfectly. The only glitch in the proceedings came when one of the guests, a heavy man, got stuck in the small opening to the burial chamber. The others struggled to free him, pulling and pulling until he popped out with a noise like a cork coming out of a bottle. The guests were awed by the sights Howard and Carnarvon had first seen that November night: the golden shrine, the huge doors, the unbroken inner seal. The opening of the burial room was a grand success.

Soon the pressure began to build again. As the 1922-23 season wore on, Howard began quarreling with Carnarvon. They disagreed on how to divide the tomb's treasures. According to the new Egyptian law, all objects from an "unsearched tomb" belonged to the state. But there was a catch: in a "searched" tomb, an excavator could keep some objects with the state's permission.

Carnarvon, who had invested so much in the tomb, claimed that since the tomb had been searched by ancient robbers, he and Howard should be allowed to keep some treasures. But Howard, who wanted to get on with his work, thought Carnarvon should give them up.

Then, suddenly, Carnarvon became ill. On March 7, he was bitten by a mosquito, then opened the tiny bite with his razor while shaving. An infection set in. There were no antibiotics in 1923, and many infections and illnesses that can be treated today were deadly then. Carnarvon carried on with his social schedule, going to Cairo to see friends. But by March 18, Lady Evelyn wrote Howard that her father's condition was "very seedy." The glands in his neck were swollen, and he had a high temperature.

The day afterward, a telegram arrived from Lady Evelyn. Lord Carnarvon was even worse.

Howard rushed to Cairo, and he and his old friend patched up their differences. But the earl grew worse.

On April 5, Howard wrote in his diary: "Poor Ld. C. died during the early hours of the morning." The time of death was 2 a.m. At almost that exact hour, all the electricity in Cairo went off.

After the earl's death, newspapers began to write about the "Curse of King Tutankhamen." Carnarvon's death was the strongest evidence for the curse, of course. But the newspapers also pointed to the blackout and the canary's death. Some of the papers began to fasten the curse on anyone connected with the tomb who died. Carnarvon's two half brothers, who died early in life, would make the list of the accursed. So would Arthur Mace when he died in 1927.

Howard Carter scoffed at the idea of a curse. "*I'm* still alive!" he would snap when someone brought it up.

Carnarvon's death did cause problems for Howard, however. The earl had been a friend as well as a patron—perhaps the only real friend Howard ever had. He felt comfortable with Carnarvon in a way he felt with few others. There were practical problems, too. Who would carry on the excavation? The concession was in Lord Carnarvon's name. Howard hoped that Lady Carnarvon would take over, but she returned to England before Howard could ask her.

A few days after Carnarvon's death, Howard began closing the tomb for the season. The treasures removed from the tomb were sent to the Cairo Museum.

By June Howard was back in England. One of the first things he did was to visit Lady Carnarvon, who agreed to take out the concession for the next season. Howard spent most of the summer writing *The Tomb of Tutankhamen*, a three-volume book, with Arthur Mace, and preparing for his first lecture. In July, he was even introduced to King George V at the king's garden party.

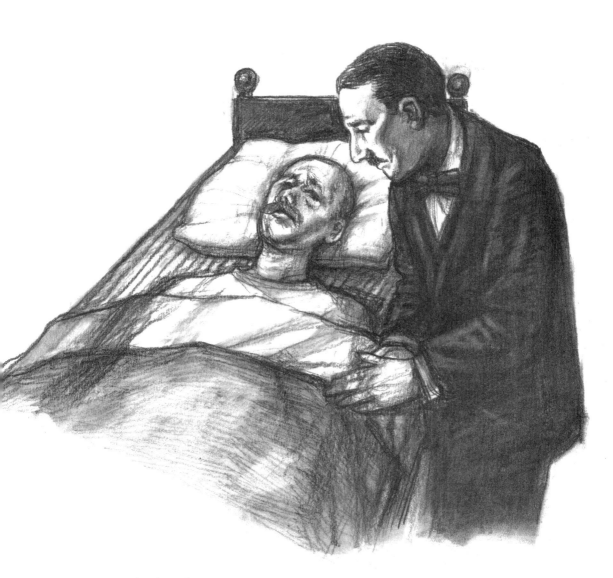

Howard's first lecture was a great success. To the surprise of almost everyone, he was a good lecturer! Harry Burton's slides of the tomb helped, but Howard's enthusiasm and knowledge came across to his audience. He even managed to make a few jokes. Many people offered Howard good money to give similar lectures. Now that he knew he could do it, he arranged a tour of the United States and Canada in the summer of 1924.

By the time Howard returned to the valley in the fall, Egypt had moved a long way toward independence. They had a new king and a new constitution. Their first election was scheduled for early 1924. Egyptians were feeling very proud of their country—and very sensitive about the control England still had over them.

Howard didn't realize how these changes would affect his work at the tomb. At first everything went smoothly. He signed an agreement with the Antiquities Service and the Egyptian Department of Public Works. But no sooner had work begun at the tomb than letters from Cairo arrived dictating other arrangements. Howard went back to Cairo several times to deal with what he called "shilly-shallying."

Between trips to the capital, he supervised the removal of the golden shrines in the burial room. It was a tricky job. There was little room to move, and the ancient wooden parts of the shrines were heavy and hard to pull apart. But Howard enjoyed solving problems like these. A fellow archaeologist described Howard as "a near genius in the practical methods of excavation."

By early January, the parts of the two outer shrines had been removed. Inside was a huge stone sarcophagus, a giant coffin with a carved surface. The lid was so heavy it could be lifted only with a block and tackle, a kind of pulley system.

Egyptian kings were usually buried in a number of coffins, one within the other. The coffins would be inside the sarcophagus, Howard knew. Howard arranged for Egyptian officials and some of his archaeologist friends to watch the raising of the sarcophagus lid on February 12. Egyptian newsmen would get a look at what was inside the sarcophagus on the following day.

During this stressful time, Howard argued with his old friend Arthur Callender, who resigned in January.

Since so few were invited to watch the opening of the sarcophagus, many important people were disappointed. At the last minute, Howard made a small change in the schedule for the thirteenth, arranging for the wives of his colleagues to see the sarcophagus after the newsmen left.

On the afternoon of the twelfth, the audience gathered in the Antechamber. From there they looked down into the burial room. Howard, Mace, and some workmen were in the burial room itself. Howard gave a signal. The block and tackle clicked, Burton's movie camera whirred, and the heavy stone lid of the sarcophagus rose slowly into the air. It stopped about two feet above the coffin. The coffin was covered by dark linen cloths. Howard and Mace began to roll down the cloths.

A gleaming gold head appeared, with lifelike eyes made out of precious stones. A gasp went up in the Antechamber.

"A golden effigy of the young boy king, of the most magnificent workmanship, filled the whole of the interior," Howard wrote in his book. The beautiful coffin was seven feet long. But Howard noticed something he found even more beautiful: a tiny wreath of withered flowers that had been placed on the golden head by a mourner.

The sarcophagus lid was left suspended above the golden coffin as the group filed past it and out of the burial room. It was another moment of triumph for Howard. Nothing like the golden statue had ever been found before.

But the next morning, February 13, he received a telegram from the minister of public works: the wives would *not* be permitted to view the sarcophagus and the gold coffin.

Howard exploded. He went straight to Luxor, where he put up a notice at the Winter Palace Hotel. It stated that the "discourtesies" of the Public Works Department and the Antiquities Service had forced him to close the tomb. "No further work can be carried out," it read.

On February 22, a locksmith hired by the Egyptian government went to the tomb with a troop of Egyptian soldiers. The locksmith sawed off Howard's locks and put on new ones. Howard could not get into the tomb he had discovered. Inside, the heavy sarcophagus lid was left dangling two feet above the golden coffin. It wasn't taken

down until March 6, when the minister of public works hosted a party in the tomb.

Howard, more furious than ever, filed a lawsuit against the Egyptian government.

It might have been helpful to Howard to have had the press on his side. But the contracts he and Carnarvon had signed with the London *Times* had made almost every other newspaper angry. Most of

their news stories treated Howard harshly. His lawsuits ended with no decisions. Howard appointed Herbert Winlock of the Metropolitan Museum of Art to act for him in his dispute with Egypt. Then he left for England.

Once again, Howard Carter's life was in ruins.

CHAPTER 7

☥

"That Job Needs You"

On April 12, 1924, Howard left for New York to begin his speaking tour. From the first stop, the Metropolitan Museum of Art, Howard was a hit everywhere he went.

In June, Yale University gave him an honorary doctorate. The lonely little boy from Swaffam was now Dr. Howard Carter.

All this was soothing for a man who felt that he had been treated very badly in Egypt. During the lecture tour, Howard received letters from Herbert Winlock about the ongoing dispute with the Egyptian government. In May, Winlock told Howard that, frankly, many of his troubles arose from the fact that in Egypt Howard was considered "difficult." Nevertheless, Winlock added, both the Antiquities Service and the government wanted him back. But Howard and the Carnarvons would have to give up any rights to the tomb treasures.

Hurt, Howard wrote back that he would renounce not only the treasures but also any future archaeological research on the tomb. Howard wanted nothing more to do with Egypt or Tutankhamen. Winlock quickly wrote another letter to Howard. The names of the others in the dispute would be forgotten, Winlock predicted, but Tutankhamen's would be remembered—along with those of Carnarvon

and Howard Carter. "That job needs you," said Winlock. "You shall be with it to the end."

Howard left the United States for England in July. He still hadn't contacted the Antiquities Department or the Egyptian government. But he was feeling better. His lecture tour had made him a rich man. Volume 1 of *The Tomb of Tutankhamen* was doing very well, too. Howard had more than enough to live comfortably for the rest of his life.

All during the summer and fall, Howard debated with himself. Should he return to Egypt or not? The month before, a new prime minister had taken office in Egypt. He was much more friendly to England. He also knew Howard Carter. The decision was made.

As soon as Howard reached Egypt, he made an agreement with the new government. Under its terms, Howard and Lady Carnarvon gave up all rights to the tomb's treasures. Everything would belong to Egypt. On January 25, in a little ceremony at the tomb, the Egyptians handed Howard the keys to the iron gates of the tomb.

There was little time left that season, so Howard postponed the opening of the last coffin until the following season. As soon as he arrived in Egypt in the fall 1925, he made plans for another viewing. This one would involve an autopsy, an examination of the dead king's body that could reveal how he died. Howard was careful to invite plenty of Egyptian officials this time. An Englishman, Dr. Douglas Derry, would perform the autopsy. The date was set for November 11, 1925.

First, though, Howard had to open the outer coffins. When the block and tackle had raised the lid of the first coffin, Howard had seen, just as he had expected, another coffin. The lid of this coffin, like that of the first one, was made of gold-covered wood carved into a likeness of the king. Howard knew from the dimensions of the coffin that there would be one more inside it.

That third and last coffin would hold the mummy of King Tutankhamen.

To make it easier to work with the last two coffins, Howard had them lifted out of the sarcophagus and brought to the empty Antechamber. The block and tackle lifted the lid off the second coffin, and Howard saw the third one inside. This one was covered with a red linen cloth. Garlands of withered flowers lay on the cloth. Howard removed the flowers. Then, in complete silence, he and Harry Burton rolled down the cloth. A golden form appeared, a form with a now-familiar face. Tutankhamen.

Around the neck was a collar made out of beads and flowers. As Howard bent over the coffin to remove the collar, he made an astonishing discovery. The entire coffin was made of gold!

But there was a problem—a big problem. Covering part of the solid gold coffin was a hard, black substance. It was a type of oil the ancient Egyptians had used like perfume. Howard estimated two whole buckets had been poured over the coffin. The hardened oil had not only fixed the lid of the third coffin so it couldn't be raised but had also glued the two inner coffins together.

Howard managed to free the lid of the third coffin by melting the hard oil with heat from special lamps. As the block and tackle slowly raised the last lid, lifelike eyes seemed to stare up at Howard. The eyes, made out of semiprecious stones, were in a gold mask that covered the head and shoulders of the mummy.

The rest of the body was covered neatly with bandages. But the mummy, too, was covered with the black, hardened perfume.

Had the body inside the bandages survived this flood of oil?

Howard had to wait until the autopsy on November 11 to find out. When he and Dr. Derry tried to unwrap the bandages that day, they found the cloth had been stuck together by the hardened oil. They cut into the bandages and removed them in layers. Soon they began to find gold ornaments: collars, bracelets, huge amulets, gold daggers, rings—148 in all. The inner bandages, when they reached them, were damaged. The oils seemed to have slowly burned through the bandages.

The bandages were so covered with hardened oil that the whole mummy was stuck fast to the bottom of its coffin.

When they removed the last bandages, they found the body tissues themselves had been burned. Other kings' mummies had no doubt had oils poured on them, too. But their mummies had not been so badly damaged. On Tutankhamen's mummy the oils had done their worst.

Luckily, the king's head had been spared. When the gold mask was removed, Howard dusted a brush gently over the head and found

himself gazing into the face of the king he had sought for so long. The face was calm and refined-looking, but Howard immediately noticed something else. Everyone present agreed with him: King Tutankhamen looked very much like the man who was supposed to be his father-in-law, Akhenaton! Howard suggested in his book that Akhenaton was Tutankhamen's father.

Dr. Derry was able to determine from leg and arm bones that the king was about eighteen when he died. The young king had lived during a time of crisis in Egypt, and some historians suspect he was murdered. The mummy offers no evidence one way or the other. The reason for the king's death is a mystery, like so much else about him.

After the autopsy, Howard still faced the problem of getting the mummy and the two inner coffins unstuck. He had the solid gold coffin lined with thick zinc plates to protect it. Both coffins were turned upside down on trestles and wet blankets piled on top. The same lamps used before were turned on full blast. Within a short time, Howard was able to separate the coffins and free the mummy.

The inner coffins went to the Cairo Museum. The mummy, rewrapped, went to the nearby laboratory. Later Tutankhamen would be put in the outer coffin and placed back in his tomb.

That spring, Howard saw two jackals on a hill behind his home. One was a grayish brown color, like other jackals he had seen. The other was all black, and bigger than the usual jackal. He had never seen a wild jackal like it before, but it reminded him of something. Then he remembered. The statue of the jackal god Anubis in the tomb! Anubis guarded the ancient kings' graveyard in the valley.

The jackal he had seen on the hill looked just like Anubis. In his notebook, Howard wrote down all the details of his sighting of the black jackal. But Howard was not superstitious. He dismissed any idea of a "curse" being connected with Tutankhamen's tomb.

Howard was able to clear the last two rooms in the tomb the following season. One of the treasures he removed was the statue of

Anubis. It was "almost shocking in its beauty," he wrote. But he was also struck by the contents of a little plain wooden chest. It held a lock of hair of Queen Tiye, Tutankhamen's grandmother. Humble items like the hair made Howard realize that Tutankhamen had been a human being as well as a king.

For the next few years, Howard spent much of his time alone, restoring items from the tomb for their trip to Cairo.

The last items to be removed from the tomb were the golden

shrines from the burial room. In February 1932, Howard sent them to the Cairo Museum. The London *Times*, which had run the first story on the tomb, reported: "A last consignment of finds, including fragments of the great golden shrines, left for Cairo today. With this consignment, Mr. Howard Carter's ten years' work on the tomb is ended."

As Herbert Winlock had predicted, Howard had been with it to the end.

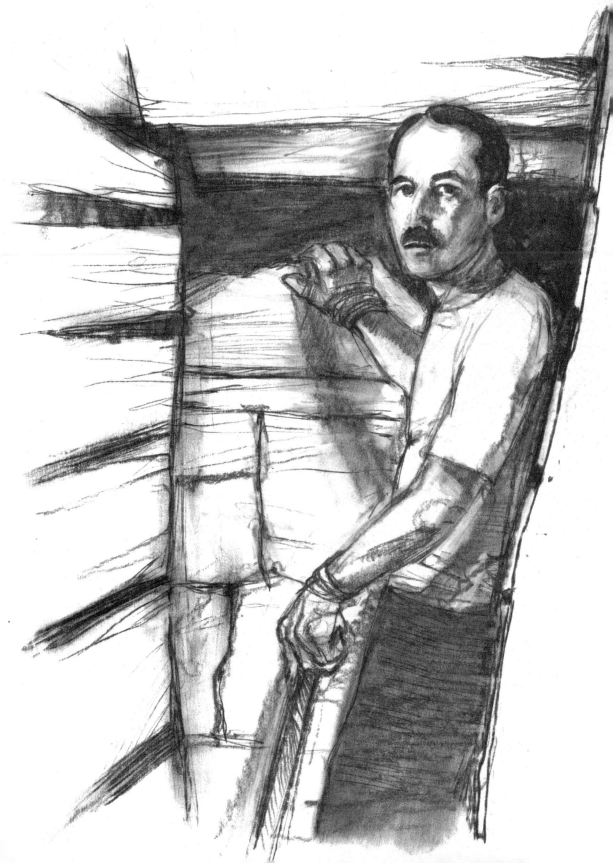

AFTERWORD

Howard Carter died at the age of sixty-five, but his work will be remembered for a long time. Howard's refusal to give up and his insistence on doing things his way may have led some people to call him stubborn. But his determination—a quality very close to stubbornness—led to the greatest archaeological find of the century, maybe of all time. Perhaps only a person like Howard Carter could have found King Tut.

INDEX/GLOSSARY

FURTHER READING

To find out more about Howard Carter, King Tut, or ancient Egypt, look for more books at your local library or bookstore. Here are a few to get you started. You might also want to check out books about archaeologists working in other parts of the world.

Behind the Sealed Door
> by Irene Swinburne
> (New York: Sniffencourt/Atheneum, 1977).

Howard Carter Before Tutankhamun
> by Nicholas Reeves and John H. Taylor
> (New York: Abrams, 1993).

Into the Mummy's Tomb
> by Nicholas Reeves
> (New York: Scholastic/Madison Press Books, 1992).

Pioneer to the Past: The Story of James Henry Breasted, Archaeologist
> by Charles Breasted
> (New York: Scribners, 1943).

The Search for the Gold of Tutankhamen
> by Arnold C. Brackman
> (London: Mason, 1976).

The Treasures of Tutankhamun
> by I. E. S. Edwards
> (New York: Viking, 1972).